What Our Readers Have Said...

"Although I consider myself a seasoned sales professional, it is helpful to have past learning's refreshed. The books were also beneficial because of the information concerning 'trends' in the sales relationship. The sales process should be viewed as dynamic since business relationships change regularly."

•

"For the particular business I am in and the type of sales calls I have, I find that the books in the Pinpoint Sales Training Series are very often applicable to how I conduct business. I would recommend them to other sales people, just not ones that are in my industry."

•

"These books provide very good concepts. It fits in well with the Bell Leadership training program that I attended in November."

•

"I use this material in these books and apply it to my customers and other employees I work with."

•

"I would like to know other topics. Is there anything on Production Management or Consultative Selling or Time Management?"

•

"These books are great tools that should be used as guidelines for our everyday

supervisory practices. You need to take the time to do a short self-evaluation when reading them."

•

"The Pinpoint Training Series delivers information that could be used in a lot different areas."

•

"I like this because I can take them with me to read at a convenient time. I feel the little time I have to spend in the office is best use on activities that directly relate to revenue opportunities. I like the short amount of time it takes to keep up with these."

•

"I prefer the self-study approach; it fits in with my schedule."

•

"My thought is that the real value of these books comes into effect when doing the action plans."

•

"Short and sweet. These books are easy to comprehend."

•

"I have enjoyed reading these books. They are relevant to today's work environment and the ongoing change in the way we manage our workforce."

•

"I do feel that these books have been very helpful to me at my job."

•

"I think a lot of the recommendations in these books are very useful, and can be applicable to everyday situations. If nothing else, it's a good reference guide to fall back upon if a situation arises in the future."

•

"These books are relevant to today's work environment and the ongoing change in the way we manage our workforce."

•

Customer Focused Selling Techniques

Pinpoint Sales Skill Development Training Series

TIMOTHY F. BEDNARZ

MAJORIUM
BUSINESS PRESS

Pinpoint Sales Skill Development Training Series
"Customer Focused Selling Techniques"
Timothy F. Bednarz

Graphic design: Monika Pawlak

Majorium Business Press
2025 Main Street
Stevens Point, WI 54481
715.342.1018 • 800.654.4935

ISBN 978-1-882181-96-4

Printed in the United States of America

Introduction

The Pinpoint Sales Skill Development Training Series is designed for targeted training and education regarding increased improvement in a specific skill or competency.

Each book within this series is designed to be easy to use, understand and apply to your job. It can be used as a basis for training individuals, as a discussion guide or as a personal training tool.

Each chapter within this book discusses a specific concept. When you have completed all eight chapters you should have a 360° perspective of the topic.

Additionally, each chapter is divided into specific sections:

- The first section provides you with an overview of the topic
- The Implications section discusses why the concept is important, and why it is important to learn and apply.
- The Strategies, Tips & Techniques to Apply section teaches how to use and apply the particular concept to your work.
- The Points to Ponder section gives you something to think about or to be discussed with a group setting. These are questions not meant to be immediately answered, but to be pondered over time.
- The Training Activity section provides you with the tools to transfer what you have learned to your job. It is designed to help create an action plan to effectively apply the concept.

Each of the topics in this series is time-tested and proven in the marketplace. They have been used by thousands of employees as training tools. Many of the users have commented that what made these books valuable, was the ability to refer to them when a problem surfaced. They indicated that they remembered reading about the exact problem. They referred back to these books and found an appropriate solution.

You will find them equally valuable as a resource in your professional development library.

Table of Contents

LEARNING OBJECTIVES:

- To understand what customer focused selling is.
- To improve performance through customer focused selling techniques.
- To apply specific customer focused selling techniques.
- How customer focused selling changes decision making.
- To apply specific techniques to make selling concepts and methods totally customer focused.

1

What Is Customer Focused Selling?

Traditional sales techniques are designed to control the customer's behavior in order to ultimately close the sale. Most buyers have become more resistant to traditional controlling sales techniques and are increasingly resentful of the salesperson who attempts to use them. Such techniques result in objections, stalls and ultimately lost sales.

IMPLICATIONS – WHAT THIS MEANS TO YOU

The vast majority of salespeople continue to be taught traditional selling methods that rely on manipulative tactics and fixed solutions to sell their products and services. Not only are these methods increasingly ineffective, but they also result in salespeople selling entirely too fast. The majority of sales are made after eight contacts with a prospect, yet most salespeople quit contacting a prospect after five attempts.

Prospects and customers have changed the manner in which they conduct business. They are more sophisticated and demanding and use more buying groups and committees to make decisions. Yet most salespeople have failed to adapt their sales strategies to match the changing and evolving needs of their prospects and customers.

STRATEGIES, TIPS & TECHNIQUES TO APPLY

The best way to define customer focused selling is to contrast it against traditional sales methods. The following stages define customer focused sales techniques:

Identify the Buyer's Needs

Salespeople traditionally present a fixed solution for the prospect or customer to buy without any real regard for their needs. In some instances, the product or service is what the salesperson has decided the customer needs without any prior investigation, or perhaps their company is featuring it and they will receive a bonus if they sell it.

Regardless of the reason, there is little connection between what the prospect or customer needs and what the salesperson is selling. In fact, most products or services are bought to solve a problem rather than fulfill a need. Therefore the fixed solution from the customer's perspective is ineffective. It is random and does not connect with their needs, concerns or problems.

Provide Information on Product's Uniqueness

Salespeople should always remember that people buy difference. In marketing parlance, the bigger the difference, the larger the space that distinguishes one product from another. If products have little or no space between them, they are automatically classified as a commodity by the prospect or customer. The only basis for making a buying decision is price.

The traditional sales approach is to explain the common features and benefits of the product to the customer. This often serves to reinforce the fact that there is little or no difference between the salesperson's product and the competition. Customer focused selling, on the other hand, focuses the customer on the product's uniqueness and links them to their needs.

Give the Buyer Time to Learn

Salespeople who utilize a customer focused sales approach give the customer the information and time they need to fully learn about their product or service and make a qualified decision. They take the time and effort to help the customer buy.

The traditional sales approach uses an aggressive sales pitch, attempting to manipulate and compel the prospect or customer to buy. As customers become more informed and sophisticated in purchasing practices, they increasingly resent these manipulative techniques. Yet it is estimated that approximately 80% of all salespeople still employ traditional sales techniques.

Help the Buyer Resolve Fears

Every buying decision is a leap of faith on the part of the prospect or customer. As such, it is natural for many of them to have fears and doubts, fueled by personal insecurities and competitive pressure and misinformation. The salesperson who employs customer focused sales techniques understands that this is a natural part of the process and works with the prospect or customer to overcome these fears and tendencies. In fact, the process leads the prospect or customer to a logical conclusion, which is to commit to the purchase, so that many of the fear factors are dealt with during the sales process.

The traditional sales approach deals with handling and overcoming objections. This puts the salesperson and prospect at direct odds with one another, mentally sparring until one side wins. This is manipulative and creates resentment from the prospect's perspective.

Provide Value and Future Results

Research has shown that the biggest customer fear is that the salesperson will disappear soon after the sale is made. More often than not, this is exactly what happens, reinforcing this sentiment. From many salespeople's perspective, the sale ends with the order, but from the customer's perspective, the sales process was a decision making process and the sale starts with delivery of the order.

The customer focused salesperson recognizes this distinction and is present after the sale is made to ensure that expectations are met and value is received, ensuring overall customer satisfaction. This is what builds and nurtures a long-term customer relationship.

POINTS TO PONDER — SOMETHING TO THINK ABOUT

1. When you sell, are you focused on your needs to get the order or the customer's needs to solve a problem?
2. When does the sale end for you? When the order is placed or after the customer is totally satisfied with the product?

TRAINING ACTIVITY — APPLICATION & ACTION PLAN

1. Examine your own sales behaviors.
2. Select the behaviors listed below that best describe your sales style.

Traditional Sales Approach	Customer Focused Selling
Present Fixed Solution	Identify Buyer's Needs
Explain Features & Benefits	Identify Product's Uniqueness
Use Aggressive Sales Pitch	Give Buyer Time to Learn
Overcome Objections	Help Buyer Resolve Fears
Close Sale	Provide Value
Move on to Next Sale	Ensure Customer Satisfaction

2

The Implications of Customer Focused Selling

When salespeople are trained in customer focused selling techniques, their entire attitude changes as they shift their focus from themselves, and their need to get the sale, to one of satisfying the customer.

IMPLICATIONS – WHAT THIS MEANS TO YOU

Salespeople should understand that the selling process is a decision making process for the prospect or customer. When viewed from this perspective, the manner in which a salesperson acts during this process should make sense and the presentation of the product or service should be conducted in a logical manner. The salesperson should consider the customer's decision making process and decide whether or not it really makes sense to skimp on information required to make a sound choice or to attempt to push the customer into a decision before he or she is ready. It doesn't make sense, yet these are tactics many salespeople use daily with dismal results.

It is important for salespeople to understand that when they change their perspective on how a prospect or customer makes a purchasing decision, it changes their overall mindset and their selling behaviors. Salespeople who use customer focused sales techniques instead of traditional selling methods will see this change happen to them.

STRATEGIES, TIPS & TECHNIQUES TO APPLY

The customer focused selling methodology is designed to closely align itself to the manner in which a prospect or customer makes a purchasing decision. The buying process can be laid out according to four key stages.

Need

Prospects and customers buy products or services for their own reasons, not for the reasons offered by the salesperson. It is up to the salesperson to identify the specific motivators of the prospect or customer. These motivators are normally influenced by two elements.

Change

Changing business conditions, competitive pressures and a host of other factors can trigger the discontent of a prospect or customer. The need for new methods, technology and materials may drive the prospect's or customer's need to change.

Discontent

Discontent, or pain, is a feeling of dissatisfaction with the situation. This can be a real or hidden feeling that is caused by something that the prospect or customer is unhappy about. It is the salesperson's responsibility to uncover these feelings of pain and discontent because they point to the real causes of the customer's needs. Often prospects or customers know they have such a need, but they are uncertain how to fulfill it.

Education

Once a need is clear and apparent to prospects or customers, they will begin to educate themselves—whether or not a salesperson is involved—about the potential solutions available. In this way the prospect or customer turns an intangible need into a tangible solution. Two steps are involved in this process.

Research

As prospects or customers begin to research potential solutions, they will also begin to formulate buying criteria that will be used to evaluate their purchase.

The primary criteria are the specifications of the product or service that prospects or customers require to perform the job or task. The secondary criteria are features that are not necessarily required to perform the job or task, but would be nice extras to have.

Comparison

Once the buying criteria are established by prospects or customers, the next step in their education is comparison shopping. They visit with various salespeople and companies to see what each has to offer in relation to their established buying criteria. This is the point where many salespeople become involved, and they are often at a disadvantage because they are entering late into the buying process. The ideal entry point is before the buying criteria are established because the astute salesperson can influence these to their advantage.

Purchase

The third stage in the buying process is the actual purchase of the product or service. The education stage provides the prospect or customer with the research and product comparisons to make an informed buying decision. There are two steps to this stage.

Fear

Prior to any significant purchase, many prospects and customers undergo a period of fear and self-doubt about their decision, which is fed by several factors. Because so many products and services are quite similar, many major decisions hinge on relatively minor differences. Since the product space is so small, buyers are often confused as to what is the best choice.

Additionally, the input and influence of diverse parties who have a stake in the purchase, including competitive salespeople, feed fears and doubts. Further, some unethical and manipulative salespeople might spread misinformation about the competition's products and services, adding more doubt to the buyer's situation. This is the riskiest stage of the sale for any salesperson.

Commitment

Once the prospect or customer has overcome any personal fears and doubts, they are ready to move forward toward a commitment. This stage is typified by negotiations to solidify the final details of the purchase.

Satisfaction

One of the greatest differences between traditional sales methods and customer focused selling techniques is in this final stage of the buying process. Most salespeople leave the process at the end of the previous stage, once commitment has been made, often to the dissatisfaction of the customer. It is at the satisfaction stage that customers feel the process truly begins; the actual product or service is delivered at this point, and they begin to use it. For the salesperson, the assurance of customer satisfaction hinges on the events of this stage. The following steps are typical.

Expectations

Throughout the buying process, salespeople create perceptions and expectations about their product or service. If these expectations are not immediately met, the excitement that accompanies a purchase can quickly transform itself into frustration, anger and doubt.

If salespeople don't carefully define and manage a customer's expectations, they can expect a host of post-sale problems.

Customer Satisfaction

Customer satisfaction is attained when value is delivered and received. Value is defined by the salesperson's ability to repeatedly meet or exceed the customer's expectations. When salespeople attain this level of satisfaction they have established a solid business relationship.

POINTS TO PONDER – SOMETHING TO THINK ABOUT

1. Prior to this lesson what was your understanding of the buying process from the prospect's or customer's perspective?
2. How does the information discussed here change your view of selling?

TRAINING ACTIVITY – APPLICATION & ACTION PLAN

1. On a sheet of paper, identify the steps that you go through to make a sale.
2. Compare and contrast those steps with the four stages outlined here to see how closely aligned your sales methods are to the elements of the buying process.
    - Need
        - Change
        - Discontent
    - Education
        - Research
        - Comparison
    - Purchase
        - Fear
        - Commitment
    - Satisfaction
        - Expectations
        - Customer Satisfaction

3

Customer Focused Selling Reduces Risk and Uncertainty

In times of uncertainty no one blames the salesperson who sells a product or service that fails to perform as promised; however, the risks to the individuals who made the purchase are high, as they often lose their jobs. With personal consequences tied to their decisions, many buyers become more reluctant to make decisions.

IMPLICATIONS – WHAT THIS MEANS TO YOU

The traditional sales approach—presenting a fixed solution and manipulating a buyer to make a purchase—is inadequate to reduce the buyer's risks and any associated feelings of uncertainty. In fact, the use of manipulative sales tactics only heightens any sense of uncertainty and may cause the buyer to withdraw rather than progress with the sales process. Buyers resent manipulative tactics and question the motives of salespeople who resort to such devices.

It is important for salespeople to understand that when they adapt their sales methods to the buyer's decision making process, they assist the buyer in making a qualified decision, influence his or her buying criteria, and anticipate every step of the sale. The need to manipulate and force a decision is eliminated when the buyer and the salesperson are able to arrive at the logical conclusion—the sale.

Fear and uncertainty play a major role in sales. Recessions and terrorist attacks have made the world a more fearful place. Layoffs, downsizing, and corporate restructuring have made many buyers leery of making mistakes that may be costly and place them at personal risk.

Traditional selling methods are ineffective at adequately addressing the buyer's fear and reluctance throughout the sales process. These fears are often so deep-seated that they must be addressed throughout the process so that the buyer develops sufficient confidence to make a commitment.

Customer focused selling techniques lead the buyer through an educational process that begins with an examination of the buyer's business and ends with complete customer satisfaction. This process leads the prospect or customer step-by-step, educating them along the way while building trust and confidence in the ultimate solution being crafted by the salesperson. This process is especially effective in the circumstances discussed below.

Too Many Product Choices

When buyers are overwhelmed with a number of product choices and options, they experience heightened levels of uncertainty because they are unsure what the right choice is for them. When all else fails and they are unable to determine the advantages of one product over another, they assume all are the same and settle on the one with the lowest price. This decision, in effect, classifies everything as a commodity, which is becoming one of the biggest headaches that salespeople consistently encounter.

Perception of Investment Is High

Under difficult financial circumstances, buyers examine their existing purchases and any associated impact on their bottom line. What may have been considered a minor purchase at one point is closely scrutinized during times of hardship. If prospects or customers don't perceive an adequate return on their investment or if they fail to see the value in a specific product or service, then the likelihood of selling to them or continuing to receive their business is minimized. This is becoming a bigger problem for salespeople who have failed to establish the value of their product and differentiate themselves from the competition.

Increased Personal Risk

One of the ramifications of downsizing and restructuring is the empowerment of lower-level employees to make many of the decisions once made by senior managers. In turn these lower-level employees feel more exposed and at risk than senior management, and they become overly cautious. They work in committees and groups as a decision making process to build consensus and spread the risk to all involved. As more companies transition their buying to committees, the selling process becomes more complicated, and the decision making process lengthens considerably.

Intangible Service

The sale of an intangible service requires salespeople to adequately educate the buyer about all applicable aspects. Because the buyer is unable to touch or feel what he or she is buying, the risk of uncertainty is heightened.

Infrequent Buying Decisions

There are certain products and services, such as capital goods or long-term service contracts, that are purchased on an infrequent basis. Since these are typically large investments, the risk associated with them is also quite large: if a mistake is made, the buyer has to live with the repercussions for a long time.

When buyers make infrequent purchases, their personal knowledge about the product or service may be limited; therefore, before the buyer is capable of making an informed decision, there exists a pressing need for additional product or service education.

Lack of Salesperson Credibility

Some products or services have an impact that is difficult, if not impossible, to measure. In one case, claims made by salespeople may be hard to verify or may seem unbelievable. In another case, the salesperson may have failed to build and establish personal trust and rapport with the prospect or customer, and, therefore, the necessary credibility has not been developed.

The methodical approach of customer focused selling provides the salesperson with the opportunity to overcome both of these problems and establish additional product credibility.

New Product

The impact of technology is seen in the development and spin-off of new products and technologies. In many instances the resulting product may not have an established track record: prospects and customers might feel that being an early adopter of new products and services is risky, and they will prefer to wait until that track record is established. However, where prospects and customers are adequately educated about the value of a product or service, the perceived risk to buy can be greatly reduced.

Cost to Switch

Beyond the price of purchase, buyers must consider the operational costs associated with introducing a product or service. These costs often far exceed the purchase price, and they create a sense of risk and uncertainty if the value of the switch isn't clearly demonstrated to and perceived by the buyer. Trying to sell complicated systems that may or may not be compatible with the buyer's existing operational systems can make the sales process even more difficult. Certainly, in these situations the customer focused selling techniques of analysis and customization have a strong part to play in the salesperson's success.

POINTS TO PONDER – SOMETHING TO THINK ABOUT

1. How thoroughly have you considered the risks associated with buying your product or service?
2. Have you seen your customers become more hesitant due to heightened feelings of uncertainty?

TRAINING ACTIVITY – APPLICATION & ACTION PLAN

1. List the specific risk factors that face your buyers and the uncertainty that each causes.
2. Determine what you need to do to minimize or eliminate the risk to the prospect or customer.
3. Identify specific sales tools you can use, such as testimonials and case studies, that can be developed to build confidence.

4

Customer Focused Selling

Selling is planting an idea in a prospect's mind and then making them feel that they originally thought of it. This is a simple concept that customer focused selling facilitates.

IMPLICATIONS – WHAT THIS MEANS TO YOU

Traditional sales methods require that salespeople select a fixed solution they feel the prospect needs and then present it. The focus of these methods is on what the salesperson is selling rather than on the solutions the prospect needs, sparking a conflict between the buyer and the seller. The salesperson is then left to convince the prospect that they need the product being pitched to them.

It is important for salespeople to understand that customer focused selling takes a different approach: rather than focus on the needs of the salesperson, it focuses on the needs of the customer. Consequently, the source of potential conflict is removed because both the buyer and seller are working together to develop a solution that solves the prospect's problems. When the conflict is removed, time is spent on more productive activities that benefit both parties instead of on stalls and objections.

STRATEGIES, TIPS & TECHNIQUES TO APPLY

Customer focused selling techniques follow eight specific steps in four major areas that are aligned with the prospect's decision making process.

Needs Analysis

Study the Prospect – The business environment is dynamic and constantly changing. The pace of change seems to be increasing more rapidly. Salespeople must understand that as changes occur in industries, companies and the economy, opportunities present themselves; it is here that salespeople must focus their attention. Changes in business conditions can create problems and dissatisfaction for buyers. In many instances, the prospect may not even be aware of the impact of change on their business.

The first steps for salespeople in the customer focused selling process are to study how changes are affecting their prospect's business and to identify opportunities where they can add value. Obviously, the degree to which research is conducted will depend on the potential value of the prospect to the salesperson.

Analyze the Prospect's Business – Change often fosters discontent for existing circumstances. The role of the salesperson at this stage is to assist prospects in identifying the degree of their discontent or dissatisfaction with the current circumstances. The salesperson assists the prospect to recognize and determine the seriousness of the problem. The answers given by the prospect to the questions posed by the salesperson are critical. If the prospect doesn't perceive the problem to be serious or too costly to resolve, they will not take any action. If the problem is causing the prospect great hardship and they perceive it to be serious, the cost of the solution will not even be an issue.

Salespeople must use open-ended questioning techniques to identify the history of the problem, pinpoint the symptoms and identify the cause. Given these clues, salespeople can then determine the complications and severity of the problem and come up with possible solutions to resolve it.

Educate the Prospect

Design a Solution – Once the problems have been identified, salespeople must shift their focus to crafting a solution that meets the prospect's needs. The formulation of the solution must be done carefully so that the prospect doesn't turn around and buy from a competitor who enters the picture with the intention to undercut the salesperson. Part of the salesperson's responsibility at this stage is to design a solution that effectively blocks the competition.

At this point, the prospect is still being educated about the problem and the potential solutions. One of the first things that buyers need to do is establish buying criteria, which is a list of features that they must have plus the items they would like to have but do not require. The salesperson can be instrumental in helping prospects develop their buying criteria and can influence them in a way that incorporates the strengths of the salesperson's product in the criteria. Using competitive knowledge, the salesperson can push criteria that include features the competition does not offer.

Motivate the Prospect – The role of the salesperson at this stage is to defeat the competition without discounting prices. The following steps are useful.

1. Salespeople must analyze their strengths and weaknesses in comparison to the competition.
2. They should develop a plan to positively position themselves against the competition.
3. They then demonstrate their superiority through the use of an effective sales proposal and presentation.

Obtain Commitment

Resolve Problems and Fears – It is not uncommon for prospects to balk and express doubts about the sale. Among other factors, the size of the investment, its long-term impact, the change in operations, and any aggressive competition can result in a stall in the process. While this hesitation is not always present, salespeople must be prepared to deal with the problem if it does occur.

At this stage, traditional methods for handling objections will not work because the salesperson is dealing with an emotional, rather than logical, response from the prospect. The salesperson can take the following steps.

1. Be sensitive to the prospect's feelings, and observe his or her responses.
2. Explore the prospect's concerns with probing questions.
3. Empathize with the prospect.
4. Discuss alternatives with the prospect.

Reach a Commitment – The role of the salesperson at this stage is to negotiate the sale and arrive at a mutual agreement. This should be the next logical step if the salesperson has followed the customer focused selling techniques up to this point. There is no need for closing techniques. All of the legwork leading up to the sale should be concluded.

The key at this stage is for the salesperson to identify his or her needs, to understand the needs of the prospect and, using joint problem solving techniques, to arrive at a mutually agreeable, win-win solution.

Deliver Value

Educate the Prospect – Even after an agreement has been reached, the salesperson's role continues. At this stage they must educate the customer on what to expect from the purchase so there is no misunderstanding later on; this entails reviewing and defining realistic expectations of product performance. Ideally these expectations should be done in writing for maximum clarity.

Once the product or service is delivered, the salesperson should visit the customer and his or her employees to demonstrate use and educate them on the best practices experienced by other customers. If formal training is delivered, the salesperson should be present during the training sessions. The goal is to ensure that the prospect receives maximum value from his or her purchase.

Finally, the salesperson should use mutually agreed upon predetermined standards to measure progress and document results received by the customer.

Cultivate the Relationship – The final stage of the process is to cultivate the customer relationship by ensuring that value is received and that the customer is completely satisfied. The salesperson must make sure that the customer gets the results he or she expected, that the product or service performs as promised, that the customer feels important and that the price was fair.

POINTS TO PONDER – SOMETHING TO THINK ABOUT

1. Do you pay attention to the details of the sales process you employ?
2. Do you see the benefits of a formal selling process?

TRAINING ACTIVITY – APPLICATION & ACTION PLAN

1. Using your competitive knowledge, create a point-by-point comparison of your products and services against your primary competitor's.
2. Focus on the strengths and weaknesses of each.

5

Best Practices in Customer Focused Selling

Most salespeople search for prospects and customers who have a need for their products and services. The reality is that approximately 8% of prospects and customers have such a need. These people are advanced in their decision making cycle and have pinpointed their specific needs. Also, they have likely researched all of the possible options available to them, and most have probably contacted every competitor they've identified. Consequently, the competition for their business is fierce.

IMPLICATIONS – WHAT THIS MEANS TO YOU

When salespeople attempt to sell a solution to a prospect or customer that has no identified needs or buying criteria, it is very likely the solution will be completely ignored. This population of prospects and customers easily represents 80% of the sales opportunity available to most salespeople. The success of every salesperson depends of their ability to sell to these prospects and customers.

It is important for salespeople to understand that if they can find one problem that these prospects or customers are not aware of and get them to examine it carefully, they will be grateful. These potential buyers will then tend to look to the salesperson rather than the competition when it comes time to commence the buying process, which effectively eliminates a price objection. If salespeople do a good job of selling, they can influence the prospect's or customer's buying criteria, yet these potential buyers will believe they came up with the criteria on their own. Additionally, the development of criteria, measurements and research will be done with the salespeople at the customer's or prospect's side. This is how salespeople effectually earn their commission.

STRATEGIES, TIPS & TECHNIQUES TO APPLY

Since the majority of sales opportunities are with prospects and customers who are not aware of their problems and issues, the best practices in customer focused selling must reside in the research and analysis stages of the process. This lesson will focus on the research; a later lesson will focus on analysis.

Research and analysis are where the astute salesperson can identify the potential opportunity and examine the seriousness of the problem alongside the prospect or customer. Without this critical foundation, the rest of the process would be ineffective and fruitless.

There are several steps, discussed below, that salespeople need to take when developing a comprehensive background probe of the prospect or customer.

Use Open-Ended Questions Only

At this stage of the selling cycle, it is not the responsibility of the salesperson to tell the prospect or customer anything: their sole responsibility is to gather information. Rather, it is the prospect or customer who should be explaining his or her situation to the salesperson. Seasoned and experienced salespeople often find it difficult to show this type of restraint within a vertical market because they feel they have heard it all before and would rather jump into the conversation and display their expertise. However, these individuals should resist such an urge and instead use their expertise to formulate questions that allow the prospect or customer to personally reflect on their own situation. The effort to keep questions open so that the potential buyer can do the talking is the first step in earning and establishing the prospect's or customer's confidence.

Avoid Problems with Non-Threatening Questions

Early in the sales cycle the goal of the salesperson should be to set the prospect or customer at ease with non-threatening questions. The key is to get him or her to relax and open up. Producing this climate is a universal problem for salespeople.

A common experience reported by salespeople is that their prospects or customers are satisfied with their existing vendor. The reality in many cases is that the prospect or customer is being untruthful with the salesperson. In most circumstances, the salesperson forces the unfavorable answer by using a common question like, "Do you have problems with your current supplier?" This question invites a simple "no" response, which destroys the purpose of the salesperson. The question is confrontational and places the prospect or customer in a difficult situation; it can make them feel that by answering they are making a commitment they are not yet prepared to make. Rather than use this question, salespeople can accomplish the same objective by asking two alternative questions: What do you like about your current supplier? What don't you like about your current supplier?

An effective tool for salespeople is a questionnaire that creates a list of problem-related questions that they can refer to during this critical stage. In this manner, carefully crafted questions can be developed and used to achieve desired outcomes.

Focus Questions on the Salesperson's Strengths

This is the most important aspect of the research phase because this is when the salesperson applies his or her strengths to the open-ended questions. Every organization has a series of key strengths that are reflected throughout the organization, including in the products or services that are being sold. At this stage, salespeople need to formulate their questions so that the prospect or customer begins to focus on their company's unique strengths. The purpose is to create a desire in the potential buyer for the things that the salesperson can offer but that the competition cannot. Since most products or services are similar, major sales often hinge on minor differences. The mark of a successful salesperson is to get the prospect or customer to desire some of these minor differences and to make the potential buyer believe that it was his or her idea in the first place.

Request Any Other Pertinent Information

As a conclusion to the research phase, salespeople should always ask potential buyers if they think there is anything else that might be pertinent to the conversation. Since salespeople can't read the prospect's or customer's mind, this is an effective closing question. If there is additional information not previously discussed or if there are points that the potential buyer wishes to clarify, this is the time when most will provide the salesperson with additional information. If not, the prospect or customer gives the salesperson the signal to move on.

POINTS TO PONDER — SOMETHING TO THINK ABOUT

1. How much depth do you feel is sufficient for developing a background probe?
2. How carefully do you formulate your questions so as to not immediately confront your prospects or customers?

TRAINING ACTIVITY — APPLICATION & ACTION PLAN

Identify the three or four biggest strengths of your company.

6

Avoiding the Pitfalls of Customer Focused Selling

While customer focused selling is a logical selling process, it does have potential pitfalls and problems that salespeople must recognize and avoid. Pitfalls are often encountered early in the sales process and can be pinpointed in the analysis stage.

IMPLICATIONS — WHAT THIS MEANS TO YOU

The analysis stage of customer focused selling is a critical step that salespeople cannot afford to shorten or eliminate. This step allows the salesperson to develop the unidentified opportunities available to the prospect or customer, and it assists him or her in seeing the ramifications and consequences of not dealing with any potential problems.

It is important for salespeople to understand and fully comprehend that consequences are strong motivators. While value is what a salesperson hopes to ultimately deliver, it is the potential consequences that can motivate a prospect or customer to act, especially if what results is an additional cost.

STRATEGIES, TIPS & TECHNIQUES TO APPLY

During the analysis stage of the customer focused selling process, salespeople should begin to explore the problems experienced by the prospect or customer. In the research stage, problems were generally ignored to place the prospect or customer at ease, but during this stage the salesperson needs to focus on these difficult areas. Unfortunately, the analysis stage is where many salespeople falter. To avoid failure, the salesperson must only ask questions, withholding any comments on the potential buyer's responses. It is essential that the prospect or customer tell *their* story. Again, the use of open-ended questions is essential, and they should follow a specific sequence.

Identifying Probes

The first series of questions focuses on the problems prospects or customers may be experiencing. They should focus on the challenges, difficulties or frustrations a prospect or customer may be experiencing. Asking about specific problems or using the word "problem" should be avoided because most prospects and customers will interpret it as the salesperson being aggressive. As an alternative, salespeople should use relatively neutral words (e.g., concern, difficulty, obstacle, challenge).

Developing Probes

Once a potential problem is identified, salespeople should develop it further with a series of probes that explore the problem and consequences a bit further. These types of questions may be: What happens if…? or, What happens when…? Additionally, asking the standard journalist's questions of Who, What, When, Where, Why, and How is effective in developing further information about the potential impact of the problem.

Impact Probes

Prospects and customers are not going to make any changes until they are motivated to do so. If a problem is perceived to be minor or have no consequences, there is no motivation to change. But if the salesperson can demonstrate the sources of pain and discontent, they can motivate the prospect of customer to change.

The purpose of impact probes is to question the prospect or customer about the consequences and ramifications of the situation if it remains unchanged. The more the salesperson can help prospects or customers quantify their pain in financial terms, the more motivated they will be to consider another alternative.

Once salespeople have gone through this sequence and allowed the prospect or customer to talk, they will have identified an opportunity while simultaneously planting the idea in the potential buyer's mind that there is a need to change. When prospects or customers think that it is their own idea, they will be more motivated to act.

With this potential for success in mind, discussed below are several possible pitfalls that salespeople must be cognizant to avoid in relation to the analysis process.

Leading the Prospect

Salespeople must allow the prospect or customer to lead the conversation. They *can* direct it with open-ended questions, but the overuse of closed-ended questions can lead the conversation where the salesperson wants to go without gathering the required information from the potential buyer.

Being Aggressive

Salespeople must walk the fine line between being helpful and obnoxious. Questions must be tactfully phrased so as not to be offensive and place the prospect or customer on the defensive. Utilizing the aforementioned journalist's questions can help salespeople to avoid this tendency.

Becoming Emotional

As salespeople successfully use probing techniques, they will likely observe the prospect or customer becoming uncomfortable as problems and consequences are uncovered. At the same time, salespeople often get excited over their successful use of the customer focused sales technique, and they may appear to be celebrating their success. Where possible, however, salespeople should contain their joy and mimic the expressions of the prospect or customer.

Focusing on Needs

As prospects and customers begin to identify specific needs, it is easy for salespeople to become involved in the conversation, discussing how to meet those needs. This is a premature tendency that salespeople must control. The development of needs and possible solutions is most appropriate later in the process when the facts are completely gathered and a unique solution is crafted.

Putting Prospect or Customer on the Defensive

Another pitfall that salespeople stumble into during this stage is to probe a little too deeply and thus bring the potential buyer to ridiculous conclusions just to make a point. The salesperson's enthusiasm can trigger questions that may be considered "low blows," which causes the prospect or customer to go on the defensive. These tactics should be avoided at all costs.

Not Thinking Before Probing

The probing sequence is a powerful way of influencing the prospect or customer. Salespeople must take care not to identify problems that they cannot fix. The focus of their probes should be on areas that are well served by the salesperson's products and services.

Failing to Probe In-Depth

A tendency many salespeople have is that they fail to probe in-depth. They are afraid to ask questions out of a concern for the prospect or customer and fail to get the necessary facts and information. Unique solutions require that the salesperson fully explore the problems in a professional and ethical manner with the potential buyer.

Not Focusing on One Problem at a Time

As salespeople apply these techniques it is not uncommon to uncover multiple problems. Salespeople should address them one at a time to avoid confusing any issues for the prospect or customer. When salespeople focus on a single problem, the potential buyer often remains focused as well.

POINTS TO PONDER — SOMETHING TO THINK ABOUT

1. How deeply do you probe? Do you back off out of fear of offending the prospect or customer?
2. How personally aggressive do you get in your questioning? Do you have a tendency to put a prospect or customer on the defensive?

TRAINING ACTIVITY — APPLICATION & ACTION PLAN

Develop a profile of your typical customer; where possible, brainstorm with other associates.

1. Using identifying probes, pinpoint potential problems.
2. Using developing problems, explore the extent of the problems.
3. Using impact probes, identify the consequences of the problems.

7

Triggering Points in the Customer Focused Sales Cycle

The customer focused selling cycle is precise and requires salespeople to proceed to the next stage of the process only after each stage is completed and the prospect's or customer's commitment is obtained. To be successful, salespeople cannot afford to short-circuit the process.

IMPLICATIONS — WHAT THIS MEANS TO YOU

Customer focused selling is effective because it follows a logical sequence that is aligned with the way potential buyers make decisions, and each step builds upon the previous step. If prospect or customer commitment to move on to each successive step is not attained, it tells the salesperson that he or she needs to do additional work before commencing.

It is important for salespeople to understand that this is a process that leads the prospect or customer to a logical conclusion—the sale. It is difficult for the potential buyer to turn the order down when he or she has repeatedly agreed with the salesperson and has committed to progress every step of the way. The process is also extremely effective because it goes beyond the sales process to ensure that value and customer satisfaction are conveyed to the buyer.

STRATEGIES, TIPS & TECHNIQUES TO APPLY

Confirmation Stage

Once salespeople have effectively conducted their research and analysis, things should become clear to them. At this point the prospect or customer should not only be ready for change but also should have a sense of urgency to make the changes. This stage's purpose is to verify the salesperson's understanding of the potential buyer's problem and to ask, "Are you committed to make a change?" This is a trial attempt at closing to make sure progress is on track. If the prospect or customer does not answer in the affirmative, then salespeople must explore alternatives. Only after obtaining the potential buyer's agreement can the sale move forward.

Requirement Stage

This is the point in the sales cycle where the customer's needs are defined. Together with the potential buyer, the salesperson should list all needs and classify them as either "must have" primary requirements or "nice to have" secondary requirements. The prospect or customer can prioritize what is most important to him or her.

Specification Stage

Quite often potential buyers are vague about the specifics they require. It is important for the salesperson to ask probing questions that clarify and, where possible, quantify what is important to the prospect or customer. In this manner the salesperson is able to convert the prospect's or customer's requirements into specifications. They can also influence the potential buyer to select specifications that closely match the strengths of the salesperson's product or service. Once this is concluded, salespeople must seek a commitment to these specifications from the prospect or customer. This is their second opportunity to gain a commitment.

Solution Stage

This stage of the selling cycle accomplishes two objectives. First, it allows the salesperson to craft a unique product solution that is designed to meet the prospect's or customer's specifications in a way that makes it difficult for a competitor to move in. This solution is made possible when the salesperson uses probes to influence the buying criteria to reflect his or her product strengths.

Second, it gives the salesperson the opportunity to gain a third commitment from the prospect or customer by asking, "If I can recommend a product that addresses your list of criteria better than anyone else, would you buy it from me?" During this stage salespeople should use the prospect's or customer's own words and statements to reinforce their solution.

The Commitment Stage

The commitment stage is the closing stage of the selling cycle. However, with the use of customer focused selling, the salesperson has already obtained three previous commitments from the prospect or customer. It is helpful to review each subsequent level of commitment with the potential buyer and then lead him or her to the next logical step, which is to agree to the sale itself.

The Education Stage

This stage of the cycle serves to sum up the details of the sale. At this point the salesperson discusses and quantifies expectations and informs the prospect or customer what he or she can expect next in terms of paperwork, delivery, installation and training. Many salespeople may find this important, but, in reality, most customers fear that the salesperson will quickly disappear once the sale is made. So, rather than confirm their fears, this is where the salesperson affirms his or her commitment and demonstrates the value that will be delivered as promised.

The Satisfaction Stage

This is the most important stage of the sales cycle because it delivers the value promised. During the education stage the salesperson should have not only qualified the customer's expectations but also described how they would be measured. During the satisfaction stage the salesperson not only ensures that those expectations are met but also measures them against the mutually agreed upon standards. Once delivery is accomplished, it is important for the salesperson to personally meet with the customer and review his or her expectations, including how each was specifically met. Only in this manner can the salesperson demonstrate the value he or she delivered and affirm it in the customer's mind. Consequently, the relationship is nurtured and solidified, ensuring future orders from the customer.

POINTS TO PONDER — SOMETHING TO THINK ABOUT

1. How closely does your personal sales style match the stages of customer focused selling?
2. What advantages does customer focused selling have over your existing sales methods?

TRAINING ACTIVITY — APPLICATION & ACTION PLAN

1. Create a matrix that lists the features and benefits of your products along with those of the competition.
2. Measure your strengths against the competitor's weaknesses so that you clearly understand your competitive advantages.

8

Making the Transition to Customer Focused Selling

Once salespeople learn the benefits of customer focused selling methods and techniques, most are eager to make the transition. However, since sales are dynamic rather than static, they will already have prospects and customers at various stages in the selling cycle. While the general transition to customer focused selling is relatively easy, there are variables salespeople should be aware of during the transition of existing accounts.

IMPLICATIONS – WHAT THIS MEANS TO YOU

Undoubtedly, customer focused selling is more effective than traditional sales methods, and there are differences that salespeople must account for while making the transition from one sales method to another.

It is important for salespeople to understand that confusion can ensue when they fail to pay attention to details and the prospect's or customer's position in the sales cycle. If salespeople are cognizant of these elements, they can ensure a seamless transition without getting confused about any issues or confusing the prospect or customer.

STRATEGIES, TIPS & TECHNIQUES TO APPLY

Aside from the specific step-by-step process of obtaining the prospect's or customer's approval at every increment, the biggest difference between a traditional sales approach and customer focused selling is in the research and analysis stages.

Traditional sales methods typically present a fixed solution regardless of the prospect's or customer's needs. Consequently, when salespeople convert from one method to another they are faced with the dilemma of what to do with existing prospects or customers. The solution will obviously depend on what stage of the sales process the prospect or customer is in. Some typical situations are detailed below.

Prospect Has Accepted Solution

In circumstances when the prospect or customer has accepted the proposed solution presented by salespeople, it makes little sense to go backward and confuse the issue by going through the research and analysis stages. When the solution has been accepted, salespeople should move the sale forward and close it. However, the research and analysis stages will be helpful to identify additional sales opportunities that may have yet to be uncovered.

Prospect Has Not Been Sold on Solution

When prospects or customers are balking at the proposed solution, displaying hesitancy or reluctance, salespeople must employ the research and analysis stages. Obviously the prospect or customer is not comfortable with the fixed solution, unaware of the value, or unsure how the solution will meet their needs and solve their problems. These two stages will assist salespeople with uncovering the reasons why the prospect or customer is reluctant and will clarify the potential buyer's actual needs and problems.

Prospect Is Considering Competitive Options

When prospects or customers have accepted salespeople's fixed solutions in theory but are also considering other competitive offers, salespeople should utilize the research and analysis stages to more carefully clarify the potential buyer's problems and needs and to create a competitive position for themselves. While it may be argued that the prospect or customer has already accepted the solution, salespeople are in jeopardy of losing the sale unless they have firmly established a competitive position that educates the potential buyer about their strengths and differences.

Prospect Has Already Developed Buying Criteria

When salespeople enter the sales cycle after the potential buyer has developed his or her buying criteria, it is already late in the process. When transitioning to customer focused selling at this stage, the same lateness applies. The use of the research, analysis, and specification stages can help the prospect or customer clarify his or her buying criteria and give salespeople the opportunity to influence some of the criteria to their advantage. The opportunity is available because potential buyers are often vague about many of their desired specifications. The use of customer focused selling techniques allows salespeople to make these criteria more specific and tangible.

Prospect Is Stalling or Making Objections

If salespeople are encountering stalls and objections, then the application of customer focused selling techniques should be employed to initiate the sales process from the start. The use of stalls and objections indicates either a failure on the part of the salesperson to properly qualify the potential buyer or that the prospect or customer is feeling forced or manipulated into a decision that he or she is reluctant to make. Rather than force the sale and risk losing it, salespeople are best served by starting over and identifying the true problems and needs of the potential buyer.

Prospect Is Being Developed or Has Not Been Qualified

If salespeople are still early in the sales cycle or have yet to qualify the prospect or customer, they should employ customer focused selling techniques. These techniques allow them to identify the problem areas and points of pain for the potential buyer. At this point, changing directions in this fashion should have minimal impact on the development of the account.

Prospect Feels There Is No Need or Urgency

If the prospect or customer feels no urgency to move forward, then salespeople have either failed to identify the potential buyer's points of pain or have not developed the points sufficiently enough to be deemed serious and actionable. In this instance, the use of customer focused selling will assist salespeople with probing deeply enough to uncover the prospect's or customer's problems, making him or her realize the seriousness of the situation. Once the prospect or customer is aware of the situation, he or she may feel a heightened sense of urgency, which allows the sale to move forward.

POINTS TO PONDER — SOMETHING TO THINK ABOUT

1. What do you see as the biggest obstacle when changing selling styles?
2. What possibilities and opportunities do you see accompanying the use of a more effective selling style?

TRAINING ACTIVITY — APPLICATION & ACTION PLAN

1. List on a sheet of paper the most common problems that you encounter during the sales cycle (e.g. stalls, objections, and so on).
2. Determine how the application of customer focused selling methods and techniques can help you to overcome these problems.

About the Author

Timothy F. Bednarz, Ph.D. is CEO of the American Management Development Group, Inc. For over 20 years he has researched, designed and authored hundreds of learning and development programs used by Fortune 1000 companies.

He is also the author of *Great! What Makes Leaders Great. What They Did, How They Did It and What You Can Learn from It* (2011).

Speaking Availability

Timothy F. Bednarz, Ph.D. is available for speaking engagements for your next meeting or association event. He can be contacted at 800-654-4935 or by e-mail at timothy.bednarz@majorium.com.

Bulk Sales

Bulk sales of this book or any other titles available from Majorium Business Press. Inquiries can be directed to sales@majorium.com, or by phone at 800-6654-4935.

Quick Order Form

Fax orders: 715-342-1118. Send this form.

Telephone orders: Call 800-654-4935 toll-free. Have your credit card ready.

Email orders: sales@majorium.com

Postal orders: Majorium Business Press, 2025 Main Street, Stevens Point, WI 54481, USA.

Please send the following books:

____

____

____

____

Please send more FREE information on:

❑Catalog ❑Speaking/Seminars ❑Mailing Lists ❑Consulting

Name: ____

Address: ______________________________________

City: ______________________ State: ____ Zip: ________

Telephone: _____________________________________

Email address: __________________________________

Sales tax: Please add 5.5% for products shipped to Wisconsin addresses.

Shipping by air:

United States: $4.00 for first book and $2.00 for each additional product.

International: $9.00 for first book; $5.00 for each additional product (estimate).

Made in United States
Cleveland, OH
06 November 2026

47678352R10030